What is in the tree?

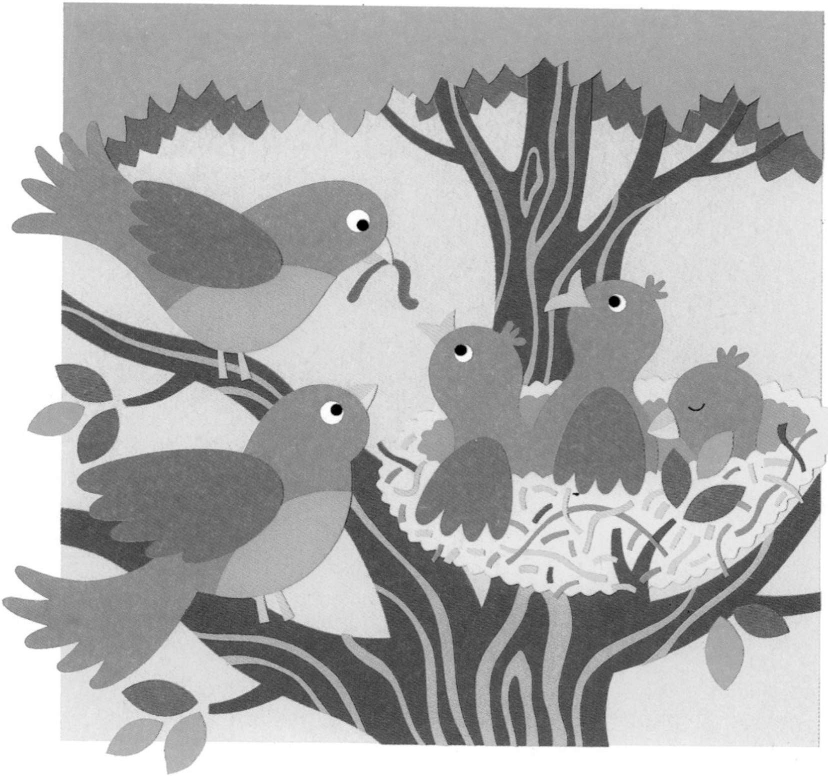

Birds!

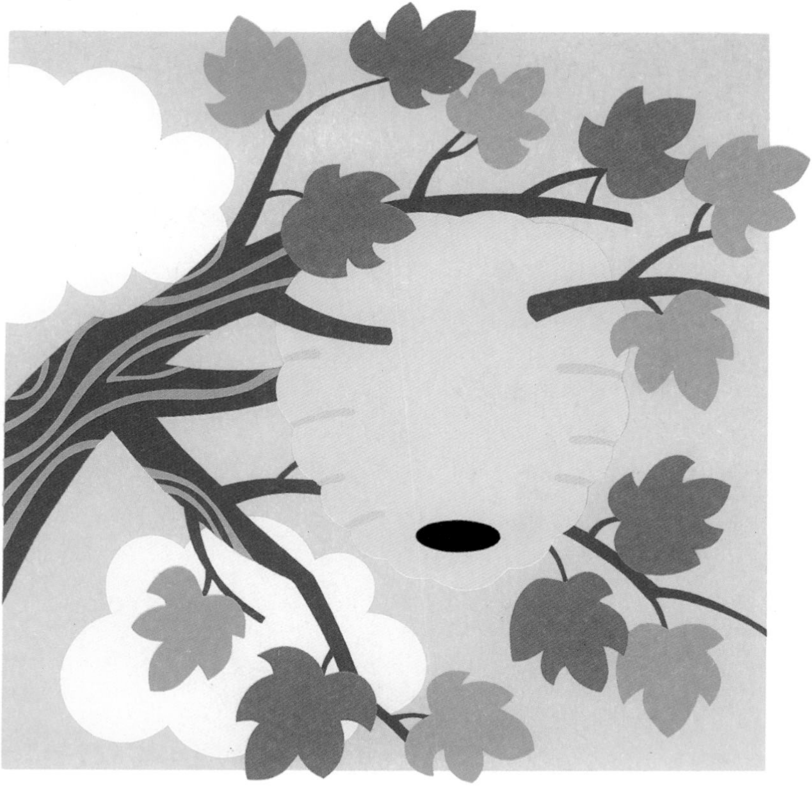

What is in the hive?

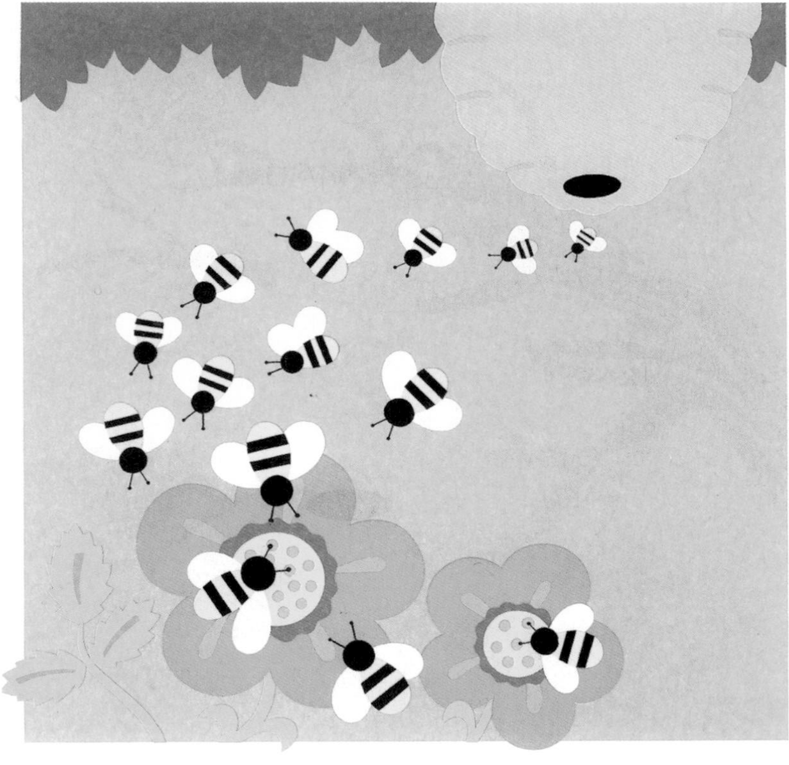

Bees!

What is in the garden?

Butterflies!

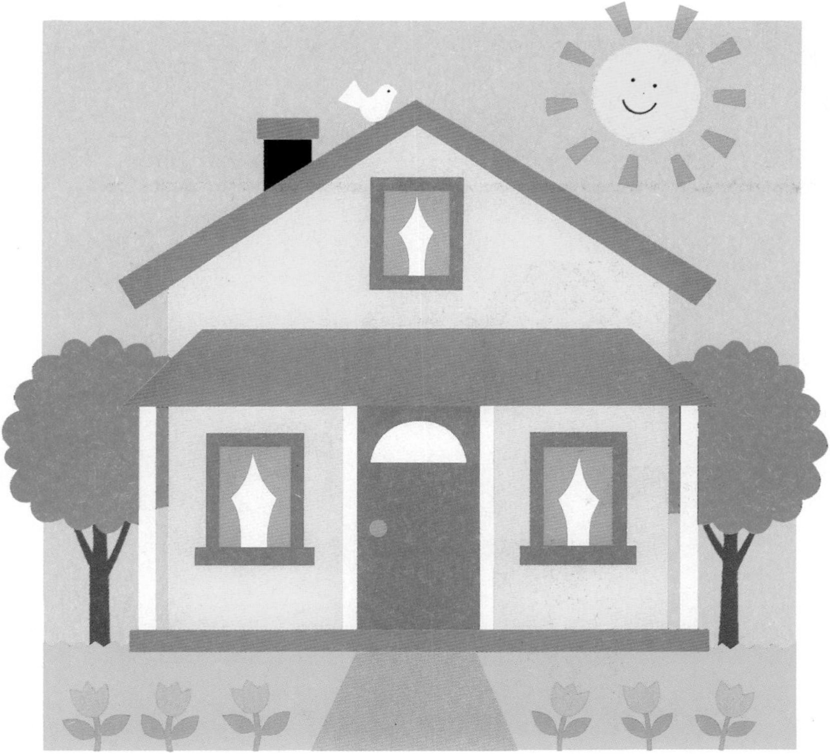

What is in the house?

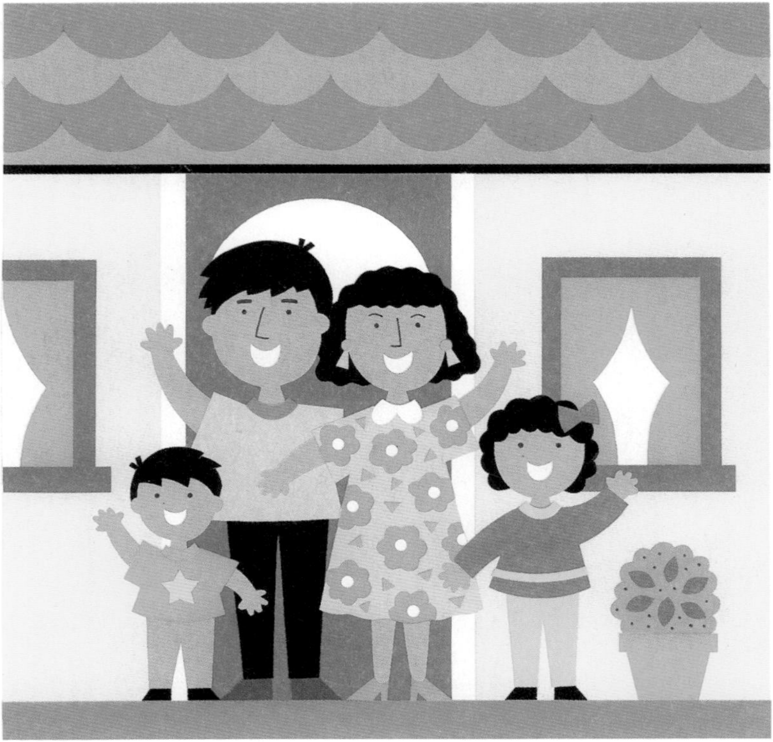

People!